T0008920

# Taxes

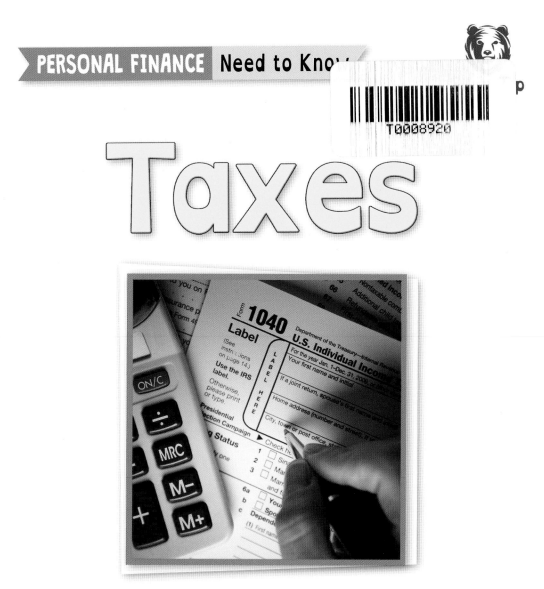

## by Jennifer Boothroyd

Consultant: Kari Servais
Middle School Family & Consumer Science Educator

BEARPORT
PUBLISHING

Minneapolis, Minnesota

## Credits

Cover and title page, © Pgiam/iStock; 5, © SDI Productions/iStock; 7, © diegomartin_toledo/ Shutterstock; 9, © Rob Crandall/Shutterstock; 10–11, © Stockr/Shutterstock; 13, © Odua Images/ Shutterstock; 15, © Monkey Business Images/Shutterstock; 17, © Freedom Life/Shutterstock; 19, © fizkes/ Shutterstock; 21, © Daniel M Ernst/Shutterstock; 23, © cabania/Shutterstock; 25, © Alexander Chizhenok/Shutterstock; 27, © Wut_Moppie/Shutterstock; 28TL, © mapichai/Shutterstock; 28TR, © tynyuk/Shutterstock; 28ML, © Iconic Bestiary/Shutterstock; 28MR, © Macrovector/ Shutterstock; and 28B, © Yessi Yun/Shutterstock.

## Bearport Publishing Company Product Development Team

President: Jen Jenson; Director of Product Development: Spencer Brinker; Senior Editor: Allison Juda; Editor: Charly Haley; Associate Editor: Naomi Reich; Senior Designer: Colin O'Dea; Associate Designer: Elena Klinkner; Associate Designer: Kayla Eggert; Product Development Assistant: Anita Stasson

*Library of Congress Cataloging-in-Publication Data*

Names: Boothroyd, Jennifer, 1972– author.
Title: Taxes / by Jennifer Boothroyd.
Description: Silvertip books. | Minneapolis, Minnesota : Bearport Publishing Company, [2023] | Series: Personal finance: need to know | Includes bibliographical references and index.
Identifiers: LCCN 2022033485 (print) | LCCN 2022033486 (ebook) | ISBN 9798885094207 (library binding) | ISBN 9798885095426 (paperback) | ISBN 9798885096577 (ebook)
Subjects: LCSH: Taxation—United States—Juvenile literature. | Taxation—Juvenile literature.
Classification: LCC HJ2381 .B625 2023 (print) | LCC HJ2381 (ebook) | DDC 336.2/00973—dc22/eng/20220728
LC record available at https://lccn.loc.gov/2022033485
LC ebook record available at https://lccn.loc.gov/2022033486

For more information, write to Bearport Publishing, 5357 Penn Avenue South, Minneapolis, MN 55419.

# Contents

# More Than the Menu

You look at the menu and count out cash to pay for a quick bite. But when you get to the counter, it is not enough. The cashier says you need more money. What happened? Your meal costs more because of tax.

Some stores build the price of tax into the cost of the item. However, most of the time tax is added on when you go to pay.

# What Are Taxes?

A tax is money that goes to the government. This extra amount may be added to your bill for everything from food and clothing to gas. Taxes are collected at different levels of government. Country, state, and city governments each have taxes. They use the money to pay for things people need.

The amount of a tax is often a percentage of the total paid for something. This is called the tax rate. The amount is decided by the government collecting the money.

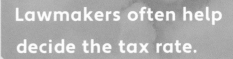
Lawmakers often help decide the tax rate.

# Different Levels, Different Needs

The **federal** government collects taxes from people all across the United States. This tax money pays for things that take care of everyone in the country. It helps older people who are retired. The money is used to keep the country safe. Federal taxes also pay for healthcare.

The Internal Revenue Service (IRS) is part of the federal government. It collects taxes. The IRS also makes sure people follow laws about taxes.

The main office of the IRS is in Washington, D.C.

UNITED STATES

Internal Revenue Service Building

State and local governments often charge tax, too. This money is used to help people and businesses in the area. State taxes could pay for roads. Local taxes may pay for a public pool or the city fire department. Which taxes you pay depends on where you are.

Sometimes, different levels of government have taxes on the same thing. In many places, there are both federal and state taxes on gasoline.

# Taxes on Things You Buy

What do governments tax? There are three main types of taxes. A tax on things you buy is a sales tax.

Sales taxes are different depending on what you buy. Bread might have a different tax rate than a pair of shoes. Sales taxes are also different in different places.

Some places do not tax things that are needs. Groceries, medicines, and clothing might not be taxed. Higher taxes are sometimes used to stop people from buying things, too. Tobacco has a high sales tax.

Stores charge tax, but they have to give the money to the government.

# Taxes on Things You Own

Another big kind of tax is one for **property**. People who own buildings or land may pay taxes to local governments. The amount of tax money is based on how much the property is worth. Many people pay property tax monthly.

Many state governments tax things like vehicles with a property tax, too. People pay a different rate on this kind of property. They may pay less often.

People pay property tax for their homes.

# Taxes on Money You Earn

The money people earn, or **income**, is the final big thing that is taxed. The federal government and most states charge an income tax. This money is usually taken out of a person's pay before they get a paycheck. Employers send the money straight to the government.

The total amount of money someone earns for a job is **gross pay**. People do not get all that money. **Net pay** is the amount of money people actually get after the taxes are removed.

# Working through the Numbers

Many things affect how much income tax people pay. How do employers know how much money to take out for taxes? They start with how much money a person makes. Then, the worker fills out a basic form. This gives employers an **estimate** for taxes.

The form workers fill out is called a W-4. It asks how many children people have. It takes information about if people are working more than one job.

Every spring, people figure out exactly how much income tax they owe for the year before. They add up their income. People also gather information about **deductions**. These are things that lower their taxes. Then, they **file** their tax forms to give the government all this information.

Paying for property or healthcare can lower taxes. So can giving money to charities. This money is subtracted from how much money a person earns. It lowers what counts as a person's taxable income.

# Too Much or Too Little?

After filing taxes, people may learn they have not had enough tax money taken from their pay. They must give the government the rest of the money they owe.

Other people may have paid too much. The government gives the extra money back. This is called a **refund**.

Tax laws change often. The amount of taxes owed and kinds of deductions can be different from year to year. This makes it tricky to plan taxes every year.

# Businesses Pay Taxes, Too

It isn't just people who pay taxes. Some businesses pay **corporate** tax. This tax is on the money a business makes during the year. Corporate taxes pay for many of the same things as personal taxes. This money helps pay for things in the community, too.

The federal government gets more tax money from people than businesses. About half the money collected comes from personal income tax.

The federal government charges corporate tax. Some states do, too.

# We're in This Together

Tax money helps everyone. It lets the government pay for things we need, such as roads and emergency services. It also pays for things that make our lives better. Public buses and parks often use taxpayer money. Everyone gives a little so we can all benefit.

The federal government spends most of its tax money on income security. These programs help people who make less money stay healthy and safe.

Do you enjoy your public park? Thank taxpayers!

# Taxes at Work

Tax money comes back to help pay for the things we use all the time.

Tax money can fix things when there is a problem where you live.

Tax is collected when you do everyday things, such as shopping.

The money goes to the government.

Then, the government spends the money to keep things running smoothly.

That way, you can continue to go about your life.

## ★ SilverTips for REVIEW

Review what you've learned. Use the text to help you.

### Define key terms

deduction

estimate

income tax

property tax

sales tax

### Check for understanding

What are taxes, and what can they be used for?

Which levels of government collect taxes?

What are the three main kinds of taxes?

### Think deeper

How would your life change if there were no taxes?

## ★ SilverTips on TEST-TAKING

- **Make a study plan.** Ask your teacher what the test is going to cover. Then, set aside time to study a little bit every day.

- **Read all the questions carefully.** Be sure you know what is being asked.

- **Skip any questions** you don't know how to answer right away. Mark them and come back later if you have time.

# Glossary

**corporate** related to business

**deductions** money taken from an employee's gross pay that lowers the amount of taxes they have to pay

**estimate** a guess with an approximate amount of something

**federal** having to do with the government of a nation, such as the United States

**file** to turn in

**gross pay** the entire amount of pay earned for work done

**income** money gained by doing or having something

**net pay** the amount of pay for work done after taxes and other costs are taken out

**property** something that is owned

**refund** to give back money that was paid

# Read More

**Lawton, Cassie M.** *Taxes (The Inside Guide: Civics).* New York: Cavendish Square Publishing, 2021.

**Sacre, Antonio.** *Everyone Pays Taxes (iCivics).* Huntington Beach, CA: Teacher Created Materials, 2021.

**Stanley, Joseph.** *What Are Taxes? (What's the Issue?).* New York: KidHaven Publishing, 2020.

# Learn More Online

1. Go to **www.factsurfer.com** or scan the QR code below.

2. Enter "**Taxes**" into the search box.

3. Click on the cover of this book to see a list of websites.

# Index

# About the Author

Jennifer Boothroyd loves helping people learn. She has been paying income taxes since 1987.